Jerusalem Dream

Jerusalem Dream

Discovery of a Sacred GPS

By

PATRICIA MARIE BLUEMEL

JERUSALEM DREAM
DISCOVERY OF A SACRED GPS

iUniverse books may be ordered through booksellers or by contacting:

iUniverse
1663 Liberty Drive
Bloomington, IN 47403
www.iuniverse.com
1-800-Authors (1-800-288-4677)

ISBN: 978-1-4917-5251-7 (sc)
ISBN: 978-1-4917-5250-0 (e)

Library of Congress Control Number: 2014922428

Printed in the United States of America.

iUniverse rev. date: 01/05/2015

For
The Lion of Judah

Contents

Part Three: The Pilgrimage

Part Four: The Reflections

Part Five: Epilogue

Foreword

Jerusalem Dream is about the quest for this promised peak experience, the Anointing, using the sacred design found in the Tabernacle.

This is not a new technology; it is not a New Age discovery. It is simply the understanding of the biblical wisdom hidden in what we call the Old Testament, wisdom that is secreted, for the most part, from the superficial student of scripture.

Those who are attracted to this topic are understandably few. However, it is to those few that I extend an invitation to experience the Anointing by way of the Tabernacle.

But does this experience require a trip to the Holy Land?

My spiritual advisor answered that question when he gave me a challenge:

First, he said that pilgrimages are the best forum in which to engage the divine forces. Second, he promised that if I traveled to the Holy Land with the deep understanding of the Tabernacle as my guide, I would surely experience the Anointing.

My question was, Should I accept his challenge?

Preface

"This should be number one on your bucket list," the flyer read. "You'll reach the peak of peak experiences you can have in this life!"

At first glance I laughed, thinking it must be an advertisement for some sort of new hallucinogenic. But then I read further:

"Each person is guaranteed to receive the Anointing by working with the sacred design of the Tabernacle!"

What is this? I wondered. *What is the Anointing, anyway? What is the Tabernacle?*

Little did I know that these questions would send me halfway around the world.

Introduction

On the bed at the Olive Tree Hotel in Jerusalem's Royal Plaza sat an embroidered pillow, black with gold letters:

Jerusalem Dream

Before I left Jerusalem to return home, I took a photograph of the pillow, because I knew I had experienced the Jerusalem dream. I knew I had experienced the promised Anointing. At that instant, I realized I was already held captive by the experience, and it was clear to me that my life's work would be to share my story.

As I left my hotel room for the last time, I paused to take one last glance at Jerusalem. I felt a deep sense of awe of this city, with its ethereal glow. It had an energy that seemed almost magical.

Jerusalem is a place of miracles. The greatest stories ever told happened here.

And now my story, small as it may be, is added to that endless list.

This book is for the willing armchair pilgrim who enjoys sharing such experiences, along with reflection and commentary. It is presented in five parts:

Part One: The Invitation
Part Two: The Preparation
Part Three: The Pilgrimage
Part Four: The Reflections
Part Five: Epilogue

PART ONE

The Invitation

The Invitation

There are many written accounts of spiritual adventures, moments of enlightenment, pilgrimages, and awakenings. *Jerusalem Dream* is, for certain, one more.

It starts with an invitation to go to the Holy Land to receive the Anointing. What is required next is acceptance of the offer—saying yes.

Saying Yes

Saying yes, accepting the challenge to take a pilgrimage, was not easy. It was triggered not just by the desire to experience the Anointing but also by a serious concern about my spiritual life.

The beloved Father Richard Rohr first brought that concern to my attention in his DVD series Letting Go, when he made reference to Ken Wilbur, author and cofounder of The Integral Life, and his perspective on the religious experience. In short, it is simply this: as many as 99 percent of the people who dedicate themselves to the practices of the church will experience no appreciable or significant transformation in their personal lives.

Reading this statistic came as quite a shock to me.

Father Richard acknowledges that, for sure, this 99 percent who partake in religious practice find moral teachings, hear the Gospel, and learn a process of spiritual formation. But ultimately, he says, religion is presented in such a way as to console parishioners—to comfort them or provide them encouragement to get through the challenges of the next week.

Ken Wilbur feels that for this 99 percent, little to no measureable psycho-spiritual transformation takes place.

What I found more shocking was his explanation that for this 99 percent, religious practices do one thing and that is to enable the *false self* to cope.

Of course, we need the false self! We create that part of our personae in order to get through our lives. It's the part of us that helps satisfy our needs and helps us reach our goals. It is the false self that we experience when we get angry or feel jealous; it is the false self that can make us feel happy one moment and sad the next. It can also lead us into addiction.

It is this false part of our nature that ultimately creates our programs for happiness. These programs are simply those activities, good or bad, we elect to engage in during our life. Most of the time, people are not even aware of them operating and perhaps controlling our life. The beloved Fr. Thomas Keating of Contemplative Outreach teaches us how to evaluate our programs for happiness, how to observe them in ourselves and others, and how such programs appearing good can be obstacles to our spiritual development.

There is, however, 1 percent of this population who do experience radical transformation in their lives, who seek to go beyond pacifying the false self, according to Father Richard Rohr and Ken Wilbur. These people's desire, their quest, is to reach their true selves during this lifetime—and what I found most noteworthy was the idea that this desire appears to be a prerequisite for receiving the Anointing.

Is Richard Rohr right? I wondered. *Is Ken Wilbur right?* Somehow, I sensed deep down that I needed to take this idea seriously.

I decided to take it as a truth. I was eager to uncover my true self, to receive the Anointing. And this eagerness resulted in my saying yes to the pilgrimage.

With that decision made, a big question arose:

If my intention for the trip was to experience my true self for purposes of receiving the Anointing, just what would it take for me to prepare for such a pilgrimage? After all, it was not just about what clothes I should pack.

PART TWO

The Preparation

My Friend with the Flyer

His name was Joe. He had slipped me that flyer.

His seventeen years in a monastery had taught him well, and he was an expert in the art of the pilgrimage.

"How do I prepare for this?" I asked him.

He just smiled and, without hesitation, placed in my hands a pamphlet, "The Twelve Keys to the Anointing," by Father William McCarthy.

"This is how," he said. "It's all about the Tabernacle, its design. The secret is simply this: It is a design given to us by God that shows us the road back home, back to the Garden. If you follow this, you are promised one thing for sure: you will receive the Anointing."

The Challenge

This left me with two more big questions:

1. What is the Anointing?
2. What do I have to learn about the Tabernacle?

The truth is, both questions present a challenge. Neither the Anointing nor the Tabernacle is easy to explain. Both are essentially divine mysteries.

Yes, we can use some facts to explain them, but the best way is to use the power of a short story.

The Anointing

Because the Anointing is a divine mystery, facts can help explain it, but a short story opens the door to a true understanding of it.

Most often, *the Anointing* is described as …

- being infused with the spirit
- revealing a powerful presence
- performing miracles
- performing an act of consecration

This short story reveals the mystery:

Kathryn was quickly escorted through a kitchen that served as a shortcut to the elevator. The cooks and staff in the kitchen didn't have any idea who she was, nor did they know that the workshop that had taken place at the hotel involved the study of the Tabernacle.

*In any event, as Kathryn walked by the cooks
and staff in the kitchen, each of them, one by one,
mysteriously slipped to the floor.*

*What had happened?
Simply put, they had been slain by the Spirit.
The Anointing had passed by!
The presence of God was so strong in Kathryn
that as she walked through the kitchen, the staff
was overcome by the power of the Spirit.*

Interestingly, the Anointing is meant for everyone. In fact, it is a sign of God's judgment *not* to receive it.

*We are all meant to walk in the Anointing.
We are all meant to think anointed thoughts.
We are all meant to love with anointing love.
We are all meant to act with anointing power.*

The Tabernacle

Like the Anointing, the Tabernacle is also a divine mystery.

In short,

1. The Tabernacle is simply the house of God.
2. The architectural design of that house was given to Moses by God.
3. The Tabernacle is a replica of the human body. Each of its components is symbolic of a different bodily organ.
4. The Tabernacle is the Tree of Life, the way back to the Garden.
5. Scripture says Jesus is the living tabernacle.

The best way to explain the Tabernacle, however, is through another short story:

It was a difficult day. Everyone seemed stressed at the office. The chaplain invited me to his office just to catch my breath.

Immediately I felt a resurgence of energy.
I shared this fact with the chaplain, and he quickly
explained that his office was set up in the design of
the Tabernacle.
"It is somewhat magical," he said.
"Try it at home, and when you walk in
from a day's work, see if you are not instantly
stress-free."
"How do you explain it?" I asked.
"The Tabernacle is a divine
architectural plan," he said.
"The body recognizes this design instantly.
Remember, we are made in the image of God.
The Tabernacle is a reflection of that image.
The rest is a mystery;
I just know that it gives us a feeling of peace,
of being at home."

A Strange Interior Design

At first, the Tabernacle was a portable house, a big tent. At the time, the Israelites lived in the desert, moving from place to place. Therefore the Tabernacle had to be portable.

Inside that first Tabernacle was the most exotic of furniture. Every time the Israelites moved, the tent and everything inside it had to be taken down and carried to the next site.

Later, when the Israelites reached the Promised Land, the Tabernacle became a permanent structure. It became known as Solomon's Temple. Today its remnants are hidden in the Temple Mount in Jerusalem—otherwise known as the world's most precious real estate.

Like any other house, the Tabernacle has an Outer court and an Inner court, the more private place. However, the furniture in the house of God cannot be found in any upscale interior-design magazine. The names of the pieces are strange but highly symbolic, representing a pathway back to God:

The Furniture of the Outer Court

The Brazen Altar
The Laver

The Furniture of the Inner Court

The Shewbread Table
The Candelabra
The Altar of Incense
The Holy of Holies

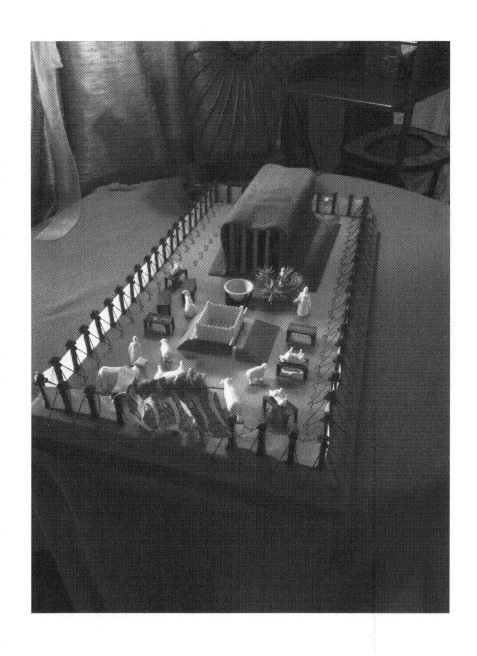

PART THREE

The Pilgrimage

Packed and Prepared

I had studied all I could. I'd reviewed the itinerary and my travel plans. I'd prepared my travel journal. My ticket from West Palm Beach to Boston and Boston to Tel Aviv was in hand. I had my passport. My iPhone was charged. My suitcase was packed.

I was ready to go.

The pilgrimage, I thought, *is about to begin!*

Getting to Boston

Though it was beautiful in Palm Beach two days before my flight, no one anticipated that the small weather system off the coast would start to organize and gain strength, developing into a megastorm with its eye on New England.

At first, forecasters dismissed the storm as no threat. I went happily to sleep that night and woke up to the rattle of shutters. The storm was at my door.

Now the Weather Channel was in high gear; the forecasters were a flurry of activity. The storm had not followed their predictions. The forecasts suddenly became dire, using adjectives like *catastrophic, once-in-a-lifetime, paralyzing*.

The implication was that airports would be shut down, transportation brought to a standstill. I was alarmed, but my friends told me not to worry. "Everything will work out," they said.

Then, late Tuesday afternoon, I received the dreaded call: my flight to Boston the next day had been cancelled. If I wanted to rush to the airport to catch the last flight out, they would reserve the remaining seat for me.

I was gone in a flash.

In Boston

I sat comfortably in an airport hotel, listening to the raging winds of the storm outside. I had made it to Boston.

The hotel lobby was buzzing with frustrated travelers; flights had been canceled, and Boston had come to a standstill.

Yet there I was.

What a way to start a pilgrimage, I thought—and just as I did, I heard a knock on my hotel room door.

Drinking Coffee

It was Judah.

"You really made it!" he said. "Let's go for coffee."

A well-known spiritual advisor, Judah would be the guide for this trip. Over a hot cup of coffee, I complained to him about the mad rush to the airport.

"That is a perfect way to start off," he replied. "A pilgrimage is not meant to be a vacation. A good pilgrimage is meant to be arduous. The fact that this one started out in an unexpected way is a *good* sign. We have evoked the spiritual forces already; the darkness is not going to let us reach the light without a fight. Hold on to your hat!"

We laughed.

Then it was time to go. Our flight from Boston to Rome was leaving at midnight.

"Let's see if we can make the next step, getting to Logan Airport," Judah said with a smile.

Logan Airport

A blast of cold, wet air met us at the door of the hotel. The shuttle was across the parking lot. I hurried into the shuttle and sat, numb, as the driver promised to turn on the heat.

Judah just laughed. "Remember, this is the way a good pilgrimage begins."

I remained silent.

"A pilgrimage is meant to take you out of your comfort zone. You had to be taken away from sunny skies, palm trees, and lovely warm beaches." He laughed again.

We bounced through the dark streets of Boston to the airport, once again navigating with the unforgiving cold of the north.

The airport was quiet. It was 10:00 p.m. Our flight had been delayed until 1:00 a.m.

Breakfast in Rome

The lights in the cabin came on, window shades were lifted, and steaming washcloths were passed out to awaken sleepy passengers.

An hour later, we landed in Rome.

"We at least have to have a cappuccino."

"Judah, we only have thirty minutes to catch our flight to Tel Aviv."

"They will have to wait for us." Judah smiled. "Cappuccino in Rome is not to be missed." He stood and addressed the group. "Come on, everyone, it is time to run."

The weary travelers got their first chance to look into the faces of their fellow pilgrims.

Arrival in Tel Aviv

Sleepy and in need of another coffee, we boarded Air Italia for Tel Aviv. Airborne again.

It seemed like an endless flight. Finally the captain informed us that the coastline of Israel could be seen out the left-hand windows.

Suddenly I felt a surge of excitement. There it was. We had made it.

Relieved the flying was over, relieved that I had made it to Tel Aviv, I happily disembarked to encounter yet another challenge: our flight had arrived thirty minutes late. It was now the Shabbat; the holy day had begun an hour before.

The airport was closed. There was no one to unload the luggage. A sole, elderly clerk stood behind the counter. He had been appointed to stay behind to assist the 195 arriving passengers. He alone would help us fill out handwritten claim forms for our luggage. No electronics could be used.

Welcome to Israel!

The overwhelmed clerk could not be certain when we would receive our luggage.

"Perhaps in two days," he muttered. "When the Shabbat is over."

Judah smiled. "This is a fine pilgrimage—made to order."

I tried to laugh.

The Hotel in Tel Aviv

We were tired and hungry as our shuttle bus pulled into the entrance to our hotel. Lost luggage was not as much of an issue at this point as our need for a hot shower and some food.

There were twenty-five pilgrims—twenty-five tired, hungry, frustrated people trying to get keys to their hotel rooms—and only one small hotel elevator was operative.

"Oh, sorry—only one elevator is permitted to operate during the Shabbat," explained the desk clerk.

We looked at each other, puzzled.

"It has to do with using electricity," he added. "Dinner is available for only twenty more minutes."

The Room in Tel Aviv

The room was small, the door would not close properly, and the open window let in the noise of Tel Aviv's late-night traffic. I was too tired to even think of calling the desk to change rooms. We were leaving early the next morning, anyway.

I sat on the bed. I had no luggage, no change of clothes. Thus far, the pilgrimage seemed to be one challenge after another.

I glanced at the itinerary, counting the days till my return home to warmth, palm trees, and white, sandy beaches.

It was time to sleep.

Reflection

When have challenges caused you to forget your intentions?

Commentary

I had prepared well for my pilgrimage—at least I thought I had. The fact is, however, I had not considered that the trip might involve one challenge after another.

Kind of like life.

The challenge of getting to Boston in a storm, the challenge of living with no luggage, and the challenge of staying in a noisy, insecure room were enough for me to completely forget my intention for the pilgrimage.

A New Day

After a few hours of good sleep, a hot shower, and an Israeli breakfast, life seemed better.

"Let's take a quick walk to the beach and look at the Mediterranean Sea," Judah suggested. "What a great pilgrimage!"

I gave Judah a good swat and laughed. "I don't feel that the pilgrimage has begun yet, I mean in the spiritual sense," I said.

"Ah, you are right," he replied. "It has not begun yet. So my question for you right now is, Where are you in relation to the Tabernacle?"

His question sent a chill down my spine.

The bus arrived, and so we ran across the street and boarded. As we pulled out onto the street in the direction of Haifa, I reflected on Judah's question.

It was then that I woke up, as if a light had come on in my head.

Of course, my pilgrimage experience to this point had been *outside* the Tabernacle. If one stands outside the Tabernacle, one stands in a world of chaos, a world of struggles and challenges. Storms, late planes, lost luggage, insecure rooms, exhaustion, hunger—they are all examples of life outside the Tabernacle.

One has to enter the Tabernacle in order to feel its power. I hadn't even gotten to the Gate.

The sacred GPS was turned on. Now I could see that this was indeed a good beginning for a pilgrimage.

Reflection

When have you experienced a great insight?

Commentary

Once I realized that I was standing outside the Tabernacle, I felt a surge of energy. I sensed that embracing the Tabernacle as a guide for my trip was like having a sacred GPS system. Immediately I knew where I was: standing outside the Tabernacle. And I knew where I needed to go: inside!

I had to find the Gate and enter into the Tabernacle.

The Tabernacle experience, this sacred GPS, can be applied to any event in your life, to any situation, anywhere and at any time.

The Sea of Galilee

Yuval, our tour guide, was the first paratrooper to liberate the Wailing Wall in the Six-Day War.

We headed toward Haifa, stopped to visit Elijah's Cave, and then continued into the surrounding countryside.

I listened to Yuval cite facts and statistics and started to settle into the tour with a growing appreciation for this small country, no larger than the state of New Jersey. As we drove on, I learned about every aspect of the land: its history, its ecology, its political stance, its hopes, its dreams.

I still felt like I was outside the Tabernacle, but knowing where I was relieved my anxiety. I knew where I was headed.

It was when we crested the top of a mountain, when I caught my first glimpse of the Sea of Galilee, that I felt pure awe.

Something was about to happen. I could feel it.

My sacred GPS kicked in; I knew I was headed in a good direction.

Reflection

When have you felt that amazing moment when you knew something big was going to happen?

Commentary

The Sea of Galilee is the historic place of the Call. It is where Christ called his disciples.

We stayed at a lovely kibbutz on the shore of Galilee. It felt mystical. But it was the next day when something I never could have imagined happened.

The Call

It was a beautiful morning, cool and misty, when we left the dock on the boats. As we sailed out into the waters of the sea, the pilgrims start singing and dancing—and I experienced the unbelievable.

While others aboard were happily celebrating, I heard a strange voice, a gentle whisper:

Patricia . . . leave the boat. Come walk to me!

What had I just heard? Was that real? It had to be jet lag!

But the call was strong enough for me to feel the urge to walk to the other side of the boat, away from the clamor and noise. And no sooner was I on the other side of the boat than I heard it once more:

Patricia . . . come, leave the boat . . . walk to me.

This time I did not dismiss what I'd heard. I recalled my intention to stay awake to every experience. Then I realized what had just happened:

The Sea of Galilee is where we hear the Call. Was this mine?

It was an unbelievable experience, but it was also undeniable. The confirmation was in hearing it not once but twice. But with whom could I share it? Who would believe it? Did I dare share it with anyone? What did those words mean?

Reflection

Did you ever experience something that was difficult to share with others?

Commentary

We all receive calls in life. What matters is whether we hear them and how we respond to them.

A call is divine guidance urging us, prompting us to go in a certain direction. The question is, How do we respond to each of these calls? A call precedes the action, the adventure.

In my case, I wanted to share what I had experienced. I needed to find out what those words really meant. Was I being asked to walk on the water—literally? Was the Call a reference to Peter? Was it a call to trust *God* more?

My desire to share the experience, to disclose something so amazing, was counteracted by my horror of being rejected, judged, or worse!

God Provides

Thank goodness for Judah.

He is a man of Christ, a man who lives to preach Christ. When he speaks, everyone listens. His mere presence turns heads.

I found it easy to share with him my experience on the Sea of Galilee. I told him what I'd heard. He listened. Then he just squeezed my hand, raised his eyebrows, and smiled.

I had not been rejected after all.

"Be patient, stay awake, trust you are being led," he advised me. "Trust that it will all become clear."

Reflection

In whom can you confide, knowing you will not be rejected?

Commentary

I was truly amazed by what I'd heard on the boat, and I was glad I'd thought to change my position on the boat to help rule out any other explanation. I'm also grateful that I had the strength to take the Call seriously when I heard the same words again.

Sharing the experience with Judah was also helpful. It reassured me. As for the precise meaning of my experience, Judah recommended patience. "It will be revealed," he said.

When I recalled my intention, when I recalled my sacred GPS system, I interpreted my experience on the boat as a call to enter the Tabernacle. Once again, my mind was put at ease as I aligned my journey with the Tabernacle experience, my incredible GPS.

The Dead Sea

We were at the Dead Sea, a majestic, powerful landscape that awes the senses.

From my hotel window, I gazed out at the sea just as the sun was setting, the great stillness of the water reflecting the clouds.

The Dead Sea Spa, downstairs in the hotel, was a series of pools. The first one held saltwater from the Dead Sea, so you floated in it. The second one was less salty, and the third one held refreshing, pure water.

After the spa I felt completely new, as if I'd been invited to some big celebration.

Reflection

When have you felt you'd been created anew?

Commentary

The Dead Sea cannot support any life. It lies way below sea level. Symbolically, it is the bottom of the earth.

To me, however, the Dead Sea was the Gate, the entrance into the Tabernacle.

It is a place of lifelessness: still, quiet, dead.

That's how the soul feels living outside the Tabernacle: lifeless, still, quiet … perhaps dead.

The Outer Court

Once inside the Tabernacle Gate, the pilgrim enters the Outer Court of the Tabernacle, representing the unconscious state of humankind. The pilgrim is now headed in the right direction—headed to the place of the Anointing, the Holy of Holies.

Enter through the narrow Gate, for the gate is wide and the road broad which leads to destruction and those who enter through it are many. How narrow the Gate and constricted the road that leads to life and those who find it are few.

Matthew 7:14

The Gate is the door to the Christ, symbolized by the reference to the Way. The Gate provides a new orientation: To face east is to be looking in the direction of man's will. To face west is to be looking in the direction of God's will; it is to travel in the direction of heaven.

As you walk through the Gate, there is rejoicing and celebration. You have found the way back home!

In the human body, the sacrum is the nerve center directly related to the generative system. It is symbolic of the gateway to life.

Remember, the Tabernacle is in the form of the human body; it represents the spiritual form of the human body. We are truly made in the image of God. And it starts at the Gate.

Reflection

Have you ever had the experience of changing directions in your life?

Commentary

This is the chance to reflect on the direction you are headed now. Is it the right direction? Answering that question is critical to your well-being, as the world seems to be descending into increasing chaos.

The beauty of entering the Gate is that when we do, we are no longer alone in the world. We no longer must struggle with life on our own power alone. The beauty of entering the Gate is that when we do, we are infused with a power that is not our own but that can change our lives.

Be aware of Gate experiences in your life and how they can be calls to embrace the Tabernacle experience.

Masada

The next day, we started out for Masada, a place I'd been encouraged not to miss.

The word *masada* means "fortress," and this one was destroyed in AD 73. It is only one mile west of the Dead Sea, at the edge of the Judean Desert. It was at Masada that King Herod built a great palace on top of a huge plateau some two thousand feet high.

We took a cable car to the top; it was incredibly steep. There we saw the ruins of living spaces, storehouses, defense towers, and the palace itself. It was spellbinding to see the remnants of a place that was once so magnificent.

The story is, the Tenth Roman Legion, headed by Flavius Silva, surrounded Masada with the intention of ridding it of the Zealots—the last remnants of the Israelites, the chosen people. Israel had fallen to the Romans, but some Israelites had taken refuge in the palace in the fortress of Masada.

The Jews fought back, but knowing they could not withstand the power of the Romans, they organized a mass suicide to include women and children so that no captives would be taken by the Romans, who certainly would not have allowed them to worship their God.

"Just who do you know who would do that now, Patricia?" Yuval, the tour guide, asked me bluntly.

I instantly realized the enormity of his question.

Would we—those of us on this pilgrimage, people claiming to be Christians—be willing to die rather than be taken captive and deprived of the practice of our faith?

For what would I die? For whom would I die? Those are key questions for all of us.

There I was, at the Brazen Altar of the Outer Court of the Tabernacle. At once I could understand why it was important to see Masada, to walk the same ground as these people who had loved God so much.

"It was over Masada that God wept," Yuval explained. "The plan for the Annunciation was born here, after God saw his people suffer for the love of him."

For whom and what would I die?

The Brazen Altar of the Outer Court is the place where the pilgrim contemplates sacrifice. It represents the human digestive system, the place where life is sacrificed to keep us alive.

It is where we separate ourselves from anything that does not support our journey to God. It is where the blood sacrifice took place in the Old Testament. It is where the sacrifice was offered, the blood of the animal taking on our sin, and replaced in the New Testament with the blood of Christ: new blood for new life.

For me, Masada was the place where I had to decide for whom and what I would sacrifice my own blood!

Reflection

For whom would you die?

For whom would you sacrifice your blood?

For what would you die?

For what would you sacrifice your blood?

Commentary

At the Brazen Altar, the pilgrim prepares to become a living sacrifice. The pilgrim surrenders at the Brazen Altar all that cannot go further on the journey to the Holy of Holies.

Again, I was so grateful to walk with the Tabernacle as my guide through the Holy Land. I learned that Masada did not necessarily hold special meaning for the others; in fact, they considered it an intrusion into their tour. There was a feisty argument with our tour guide. "Let's bypass Masada!" they shouted angrily. Yuval replied that he was obliged to follow the itinerary. Sharp words flew back and forth.

I was speechless but secretly happy that Masada, the Brazen Altar, was not deleted from our agenda.

The Jordan

We were at the Jordan River. I looked at this famous place, which was lined by tall reeds. The water was still. It was the middle of the day, and it was hot. Flies buzzed about us.

Machine guns were pointed politely toward us by Jordanian soldiers sitting across the river.

This was where Yeshua was baptized, Yuval said.

For me, this was the place of the Laver in the Outer Court of the Tabernacle. The Laver symbolizes the place of purification. It represents the kidneys in the human body, organs critical to elimination.

The Laver is where we cleanse the body, as well as the mind. It is here that the pilgrim prepares to enter the Inner Court.

You may recall from chemistry class that water is the universal solvent; it removes the toxins from our bodies and the soil from our clothes. Water is the substance God uses to break up and dissolve old, error-ridden states of mind.

Just as the floodwaters in the story of Noah eliminated the negative habits of mankind, water can purify us, cleanse us.

The Laver is that place of pouring into us the dissolving power of the Word, which breaks up and washes away all thoughts of negativity. The Laver is symbolic of the ritual bath of ancient times, the process of purification. Bathing is still something we celebrate as an act of cleansing.

Reflection

What is it that I must eliminate from my life now?

What obstacles must I dissolve?

What part of my life requires cleansing?

Commentary

The Laver is that place where we might cleanse not just the physical body but the mind as well. This is the place that prepares us to approach the Inner Court of the Tabernacle.

The act of washing or cleansing also symbolizes removing obstacles that could interfere with our communication with God.

We can practice the Laver experience as we drink a glass of water, wash our hands, take a shower, or (of course) take a bath. Certainly we can use the act of purification throughout our daily lives.

Welcome to the Inner Court

Having walked through the Gate of the Tabernacle; passed the Brazen Altar, the place we contemplate sacrifice; and visited the Laver, the place of eliminating whatever cannot be brought into the holy place, the pilgrim is prepared to enter into the Inner Court of the Tabernacle.

The components of the Inner Court are as follows:

- the Altar of Incense
- the Candelabra
- the Shewbread Table
- the Holy of Holies

The Mount of the Beatitudes

The beauty of this place, the Mount of the Beatitudes, was astounding. I felt as though I had just entered heaven.

The tall date palms swayed in a breeze that was magnificent, gentle, and soothing. There were gardens everywhere, roses of every color, and a large fountain streaming through a rock garden. And this scene was set against the backdrop of the Sea of Galilee.

I had reached heaven on earth.

It was easy to realize that for me this place, the Mount of the Beatitudes, represented the entrance to the Inner Court of the Tabernacle. Here there was the sense of peace and security I had always longed for.

It is within the Inner Court that the pilgrim enters into the conscious state of mind, the place of our interior nature, the place of the contemplative disposition. The pilgrim's soul now is in the court of the Altar of Incense, the Candelabra, the Shewbread Table, and the Holy of Holies.

The Mount of the Beatitudes is the New Mount Sinai; it is the place where the New Torah was first revealed; it is the place of the parables.

It is the site of the invitation to either enter into the deeper mysteries of Christ—or not. At this place, the pilgrim must have ears to hear.

The pilgrim must remember that the parables presented to us at this site were meant to confound us, to force us to ask questions in order to receive the full meaning. The parables require us to enter into a dialogue. They require us to be in conversation. They require a relationship.

The parables will either confuse us to the point of frustration, or they will serve as an invitation to a deeper life, that of the conscious human, and ultimately take the student to greater depths of spirituality.

Those who embark on a quest for the deeper insights will continue into the Inner Court; those who do not will remain in the Outer Court.

I could feel a strangeness hidden in the deep silence on this mountain, hidden in its alluring beauty. I had the feeling that what had happened there was so big that, in time, it would change the world.

I felt welcome to the Inner Court.

Reflection

Where have you experienced an Inner Court?

Where is the Inner Court in your life?

Does your home give you a feeling of entering the Inner Court?

Commentary

The Inner Court is where I want to live. It is the place of the conscious state of mind. It is the place where I am about to enter the Holy of Holies.

We can consciously make our lives, here and now, an Inner Court experience. Our homes should have this quality; they should be places of renewal, places like the Mount of the Beatitudes.

The Wailing Wall

We entered Jerusalem, the historical site of the first Tabernacle, the former Temple of Solomon. We were finally at the Wailing Wall, the last remnant of the Second Temple, Judaism's most sacred site.

It is a place of prayer. It is a place of pilgrimage.

Our guide, Yuval, was one of the first paratroopers to liberate the wall in the Six-Day War of 1967.

When the Jews regained access to their sacred place, their prayers—reflecting their sorrow at having been disconnected from it, at having lost the temple—were more like lamentations than rejoicing. Hence its name, the Wailing Wall.

I knew I had arrived at the Altar of Incense; there was such a sense of reverence. The women praying at the wall would leave facing it, walking backward away from it. Turning their backs on this most sacred site would be like walking away from God.

This great gesture of respect made me cry.

I had not seen such deep devotion since leaving Ethiopia, where people would prostrate themselves on the ground before entering church.

It took my breath away.

Incense is symbolic of prayer; we watched the smoke curl as it rose into the air, taking our prayers to heaven.

Knowing how to pray is knowing the most powerful force of the cosmos. Prayer is about praise; it places us into the flow of grace, a place of miracles, healing, and well-being.

The Altar of Incense symbolizes the spleen. The rising aroma of incense is akin to our red blood cells giving themselves in service of the body, the human tabernacle. Here we experience a kind of marriage of the power of the Word and the rise of prayer.

It was there, at the Wailing Wall, that I felt the divine marriage.

Prayer is actually what we should become!

Reflection

What are you praying for?

Do you pray?

Commentary

Realize that prayer is anything you are doing or thinking at any one moment. Everything we do, therefore, could be considered prayer!

The question is, Are your prayers conscious or unconscious?

If prayer is everything you do, prayer is then everything you think, everything you say, every move you make, everything you listen to.

They say that all of life is training to become prayer. So make your life a beautiful prayer. Then prayer is who you are!

Prayer is being connected to the power of the Creator. Staying connected helps us move closer to the place of the Anointing, the Holy of Holies.

The Mount of the Transfiguration

We were at the Mount of the Transfiguration, the place where Jesus was seen in a field of light, his garments glittering white.

It is not easy to reach the top of this mountain. Special vehicles are required, manned by specially-trained drivers who can maneuver up and down the steep, winding road. The brakes on their vehicles need to be changed almost every week. The constant up and down with pilgrims is serious business.

It was especially cool the morning we arrived on the mountaintop. We walked down to the church, entered its dark interior, looked up, and saw golden artwork shimmering in the early morning light.

I could feel a peculiar lightness there.

It was easy for me to identify this as the Candelabra of the Tabernacle, the humans' sacramental energy centers, which, when they are illuminated, become the wedding garment.

The Candelabra represents creation; the seven candles are symbolic of the Tree of Life. The number seven is the covenant number.

This is where we think about the fact that all creation exists in order to receive and reflect the light of the infinite source. It is a kind of mystical marriage; hence it is the place to witness the scriptural wedding garment.

Scripture says that John saw one like the Son of Man in the midst of the seven golden candlesticks, the Candelabra.

Candelabras use oil to produce light. Likewise, the pancreas uses oil in the form of human fat to produce oil for the body (soluble glycerin and fatty acids).

Like Jesus, we strive to become illuminated, to burn with life, to burn with the Word for his glory.

It was there at the Mount of the Transfiguration that I began to feel a strange sensation, as if I were on fire.

Reflection

Where have you experienced a transcendent light?

Where were you when you felt an enormous surge of energy, a lightness?

Commentary

The practice of the Candelabra may involve something as simple as lighting a candle and sitting with it. If you gaze at the glow around the candle, if you sit patiently long enough, you will eventually see a rainbow of colors. You'll perceive those colors in a new way, and with practice you will see the rainbow of colors everywhere.

Learning to see the world in this way brings us out of the density of the world. It is a practice that brings lightness into our lives. It is a practice that reminds us of the Mount of the Transfiguration, a prefigurement of the resurrection of Christ.

Ultimately, everything is made of light.

At Ein Karem

It was at the Church of the Visitation at Ein Karem that I fell in love with Jerusalem. I could have stayed there forever!

I looked up and, across the hill, spotted a lovely balcony apartment with a garden patio and wondered, *Could I spend my life here?* I could see myself having a morning cappuccino on that patio and then walking to the Church of the Visitation, passing by the bakery on the way home for fresh bread, and in the evening having friends over for cheese and good wine.

Ein Karem is enchanting.

The Church of the Visitation was, to me, the loveliest of all the churches I visited. I felt a presence there, a beautiful innocence, perhaps, since here is the story of two women of the bible coming together and praising God.

The church was surrounded by gardens, and it was quiet; there were no pressing crowds there.

It's no wonder I felt a great connection to the site. It was the place where Elizabeth cried out the same prayer that King David did before the Ark of the Covenant.

In doing so, she confirmed Mary as the Ark of the New Covenant.

This history in itself was spiritual food for me. The church was a place that fed my life's passion, the study of the Ark of the Covenant, both the old and the new.

It was there that I encountered the Altar of the Shewbread found in the Tabernacle, mentioned in Exodus 23:30:

> *Put the Bread of the Presence on this table to be before me at all times.*

This altar, Shewbread Table, is the place where you find the food, the "bread," that sustains you in life. It has to do with knowing your true identity and understanding your life purpose—your mission. Once you have discovered these things, you do not want to stray; you do not want to become distracted by external things. Once you have found your true place in the world, it is like living in another place, one not found in the global marketplace. It is a kind of heaven on earth.

The Shewbread Table symbolizes the liver, the storehouse of energy for the human body. The Church of the Visitation was that storehouse for me.

We fell out of the Garden of Eden because we ate of the wrong food. Hence at the Shewbread Table, we choose to eat the right food, food that will help us find our way back to Paradise. When we feast on the Word of God, we enter the New Jerusalem; we actually feed on light, and we become less dense, feeling that peculiar sensation of airiness.

That was my experience at the Church of the Visitation: I fed on light.

Reflection

What is the bread that feeds your energy?

What do you choose to feed on in this life?

Commentary

What we eat physically is less important than what our minds feed on, what our ears feed on. The Shewbread Table makes us stop and contemplate what we are feeding on in this life.

As humans, we are constantly feeding on something: a thought, a past event, a hope; something we've heard or read or seen. What you are currently feeding on may not be that food that will help you get closer to the Holy of Holies.

There at Ein Karem, I felt I had been feeding on the right food, the right bread. I felt energized and ready to enter into the Holy of Holies.

On the Way to the Holy Sepulcher

When I awoke that next morning in the Olive Tree Hotel, I was aware that I had miraculously managed to enter the Tabernacle during this pilgrimage and that doing so had provided an incredible new dimension to my journey. At each site along the way, I'd managed to listen intently to what the Holy Spirit may have been imparting:

I first arrived *outside* the Tabernacle in Tel Aviv.

I received the *Call* on the Sea of Galilee.

I entered the *Outer Court.*

I walked through the *Gate* at the Dead Sea.

I experienced the *Brazen Altar* at Masada.

I touched the *Laver* at the River Jordan.

I had the sublime experience of coming into the *Inner Court* at the Mount of the Beatitudes.

I experienced the *Altar of Incense* at the Wailing Wall.

I experienced the *Candelabra* at the Mount of the Transfiguration.

I experienced the *Altar of the Shewbread* at Ein Karem.

What was left, of course, was to receive the promise. What was left was to receive the Anointing.

Just how is that going to happen? I wondered. I almost hesitated to think it could. Maybe it was best just to be grateful for what I had already experienced; that was enough to be thankful for.

It was with these thoughts that I found myself on the bus again, ready to visit the prime real estate, the Church of the Holy Sepulcher. We were approaching the Old City.

We had walked through one of the city gates and were getting closer to the Sepulcher when suddenly Judah gunned ahead of us. He had recognized an Ethiopian monk who was sitting in a chair near some steps outside an old green door next to the Sepulcher.

I ran to catch up. By the time I got there, the two men were already engaged in conversation.

It was nice to hear the sound of Amharic again. Listening to the men, I felt strange, as though I were being pulled back to Ethiopia. For a few minutes I resisted leaving, as the other pilgrims had caught up with us and were in a hurry to move on to the Sepulcher.

Judah would not be rushed. He remained in conversation with the Ethiopian, and I made a split-second decision to stay with him at the risk of losing our group.

Little did I know that my impulse to stay behind with Judah would ultimately become the most important decision of my life.

Reflection

Have you ever taken a risk?

Have you ever taken the road less traveled?

Have you ever made a split-second decision that would change your life?

Commentary

I had been well advised that to make the pilgrimage a transformative one, I might have to risk losing the group. So I was prepared, after only a few seconds of deliberation, to remain with Judah.

When I look back on that decision, my mind is boggled at the thought of what the consequences would have been had I not decided to stay.

Hence I believe we need to have faith in the Holy Spirit and recognize when the wind is blowing and prompting us to move in a new direction. We must have the courage to act even when that action does not seem to fit in with our life's itinerary and plans.

An Ethiopian Presence

Judah introduced me to the Ethiopian monk, who blessed me, held my hand, and continued his conversation with Judah. This was a moment that gave me great pause. I realized it in an instant: we were meant to be there.

My mind raced back in time.

The Ethiopian presence at the place of the Sepulcher has been unbroken for some fifteen hundred years. The Ethiopian monastery is actually part of the Church of the Holy Sepulcher. However, it is not ornate. There is no gold or silver; there is no beautiful décor. The place is more like a rock-hewn cave: simple, powerful in its silent, unadorned witness.

It is said that King Solomon gave this parcel of land to the Queen of Sheba as a wedding present. And the story of King Solomon and the Queen of Sheba, who was from Ethiopia, involves the Ark of the Covenant.

The story of the Ark of the Covenant includes the Tabernacle.

And the Ark is kept in the Holy of Holies of the Tabernacle, the place of the Anointing.

My mind was racing with thoughts, memories, and all that I had studied for the last twenty-five years. It was as if everything was converging, collapsing into a few moments of earth time, a few moments of life experience. I stood still, attempting to reconnect with what was in front of me: Judah still conversing with the Ethiopian monk. The others had long left us.

Reflection

When has your life focus connected to one particular moment in time?

Can you identify a moment when you felt God's guidance and it took you away from the crowd?

Commentary

So what was so special about standing in the Ethiopian monastery in Jerusalem? After all, if you didn't know its history, you would pass it quickly—like most people do in their rush to the big Church of the Holy Sepulcher.

But it was at that Ethiopian monastery that one of the most famous stories of all time took place—that is, the story of Solomon and Sheba, which eventually would give shape to an interesting aspect of our Christian history.

Carl Jung saw the story of Solomon and Sheba as a source for teaching about archetypes and icons and how they can help us understand our lives. In brief, the story of Solomon and Sheba goes like this:

King Solomon was going to build a grand temple to house the Ark of the Covenant. It would be a permanent tabernacle, one made of stone and lined with gold, jewels, and fine tapestries. He sent out invitations to all the world (as he knew it), encouraging other rulers as well as commoners to participate in this great building project.

The Queen of Sheba lived in the south, most likely in Ethiopia. Today Sheba is a living icon in Ethiopian history, frequently featured in paintings on walls of restaurants, stores, and churches. She seems to be everywhere. You can still see the ruins of her palace swimming pool.

When I lived in Ethiopia, I was captivated by this magnificent woman who changed history and who is so often forgotten, even though the scriptures indicate she will stand with Jesus at judgment time.

King Solomon sent invitations out to the far corners of the earth to come to Jerusalem. The Queen of Sheba received one such invitation.

Her close advisor kept encouraging her to go. He had been there and was impressed by Solomon's wisdom, amazed at his palace, and awed by his plans to build the most splendid of temples.

Inspired by the stories her advisor told her, the queen decided she would go. She, too, was drawn to King Solomon's wisdom, and she was most interested in his religion.

The story of Sheba's journey is chronicled in the Bible. She left her home country with a caravan of hundreds of camels loaded with incredible gifts for King Solomon and his new building project. It is said that as soon as King

Solomon saw her, he fell in love with her. He wanted to marry her, but she was not sure. She was intrigued by his wisdom, however, and mesmerized by his religion. She opted to stay at his palace for a long time. She loved being in Jerusalem.

Despite her failure to reciprocate his feelings, Solomon kept on desiring Sheba, and he decided that he was going to have her.

He came up with a rather crafty plan.

He had his cooks make her an exquisite Ethiopian dinner. The food was wonderful but incredibly spicy, so spicy that the queen became very thirsty. Solomon was careful not to serve any drink with the meal. He kept the conversation going so the queen did not really notice the absence of water or wine. She greatly enjoyed the dinner.

As part of the dinner conversation, Solomon promised Sheba that he would never take her by force. There was only one rule, he said, and if she broke it, he would claim the right to marry her.

Sheba was never to steal anything precious from his palace.

Without hesitation, Sheba agreed. Solomon quietly chuckled.

That night, after the very, very spicy dinner, Sheba looked around the palace for some water. She couldn't find any.

She was very thirsty.

Finally she saw all the water jugs, which had been placed around Solomon's bed. Carefully she crept up to his bed to get some water from a jug. Just as she finished drinking, the king grabbed her arm and said, "You have stolen something most precious to me and that is water." He grinned. "You have broken the one rule."

"Yes, I suppose I have," Sheba said.

And so Sheba and Solomon were married.

For a wedding present, Solomon gave Sheba an exquisite ring as well as land next to the palace, which today is the site of the Ethiopian monastery.

Not long after their marriage, Sheba announced to Solomon that she was pregnant and that it was time for her to return to Ethiopia. Solomon was saddened by her departure, but the fact was that the queen had been absent from her native land for some time. When she arrived home, Sheba gave birth to a boy named Menelik, which means "son of a king."

When Menelik turned twenty-one, he asked his mother, the Queen of Sheba, for permission to go to Jerusalem and visit his father, King Solomon. The queen slipped off the wedding ring that the king had given her, and she gave it to Menelik so that King Solomon would receive him as his own.

When Menelik reached Jerusalem, the people were shocked to see him. He was just a younger version of his father. Menelik apparently stayed many years there with King Solomon, learning about Judaism and the Tabernacle.

Finally it was time for Menelik to return home to his own land and to his mother. King Solomon, sorry to see such a favored son leave, decided to give him the most important of his treasures. It is said that Solomon entrusted the Ark of the Covenant to Menelik, who took it to his own land as a gift to his mother, the Queen of Sheba. The king also sent the firstborn of every high priest in Jerusalem to accompany and protect Menelik on his journey home. They were to stay in Ethiopia, teach the people about Judaism, and be the custodians of the Ark.

So that is how the Ark ended up in Ethiopia, which still claims to have the Ark in its possession today. Is this also how the priestly class migrated to Ethiopia? And is it how the Tribe of Judah came to Ethiopia?

That tribe is of utmost importance, because it is the one that gave rise to Christ. It is also written that the Tribe of Judah "hath prevailed to open the book and to loose the seven seals thereof"(Rev. 5:5).

All these thoughts raced through my mind as I stood there listening to Judah and the Ethiopian monk. I realized I was standing on holy ground.

This was the place where King Solomon once stood. This was the place where the Queen of Sheba once walked.

A Life-Altering Detour

The monk invited us inside his monastery.

As Judah and I walked up the steps to the old, worn green door, I could not help but recall the importance of the Queen of Sheba and King Solomon, whose lives are connected in history to the Ark of the Covenant.

We followed the monk inside. The place was dark and narrow, like a cave. There was a heavy scent of incense.

The monk pointed to a huge painting hanging on a stone wall. Judah and I eyed each other in disbelief. It was a portrait of the Queen of Sheba and King Solomon with the Ark of the Covenant.

Reflection

When has a painting, book, or movie inspired a moment of life reflection for you?

What was your response to that moment?

Commentary

What made this picture so amazing? It was the Ark of the Covenant, the treasure of all treasures. Even today there are people searching vigorously for its whereabouts.

If we do not understand the significance of the Ark, the story of Solomon and Sheba remains a mere love story. It is because of the Ark of the Covenant that their relationship became one of the greatest stories of all time.

The Bible says that God gave Moses precise measurements for building the ark, which was made of acacia wood and plenty of gold. It housed the Rod of Aaron, the Tablets of the Law, and the Golden Vase of Manna, all of which would point to the New Testament.

More simply, the ark was considered God's footstool, the place where he would reside in the Tabernacle. It is there that God promised to dwell and be present to his people, the Israelites. The Bible says that God appeared on the "mercy seat" of the ark as a cloud by day and as fire by night.

This Ark of the Covenant was built of earthly materials and prefigured the living ark, which would be Christ.

The ark was kept in the Holy of Holies, where one receives the promised Anointing.

Standing before the Ark

We were ushered through a winding passage. Along the way we saw monks in silent prayer, their heads covered, prayer books and crosses in their hands.

Never before had I witnessed such sanctity, such peace, such a presence of the holy.

The monk stopped by a tabernacle and pulled aside a veil. Behind the veil was the sacred replica of the Ark.

How is this possible, that in Jerusalem I am standing before the Tabernacle, the Holy of Holies, the Ark of the Covenant?

As I wondered how I had arrived at this place, a monk offered me a piece of corsi, spicy Ethiopian bread. Tasting it, I suddenly felt all my senses being saturated in the presence of that which was holy.

It was ...

the *touch* of the blessing by the monk.

the *sound* of holy silence.

the *sight* of the Holy of Holies, the ark.

the *smell* of the incense.

the *taste* of the spiced bread.

It was a full anointing!

Here in the poorest of places, the humblest of places, the quietest of places, the most hidden of places, the most secret of places, I was overcome with an indescribable joy.

Tears came to my eyes.

God had kept his extraordinary promise—a promise which was delivered in the most unbelievable, most amazing way.

As I looked around me, I saw to my amazement that everything seemed to be bathed in a soft light, a glow. I felt a love for everyone I saw, a love unlike anything I had ever experienced. It was as if I were in another world, a place of joy, light, and everlasting peace.

Reflection

When in your life have you attained your heart's desire?

When has life surprised you with something far greater than you ever could have imagined?

Commentary

It seemed like an eternity, but finally there we were, Judah and I, outside the Ethiopian monastery, walking again among the crowds to the bigger Church of the Holy Sepulcher.

We pushed our way through the dense crowds to reconnect with our group.

The Church of the Holy Sepulcher is the highlight of any pilgrimage to the Holy Land. This was supposed to be the peak experience of our trip. It was big, *huge*, full of gold candelabras, silver oil lamps, paintings, and elaborate tapestries.

It was hard to find the sacredness in the pressing crowd, with all the flashing cameras and the people talking and shoving their way forward.

As for me, my peak experience as a pilgrim to the Holy Land was next door, in a quiet, forgotten corner of the Sepulcher—the Ethiopian monastery, where I had experienced the immense presence of God.

The place of my Anointing.

I could only smile. I had received the gift of all gifts!

PART FOUR

The Reflections

Gifts of the Anointing

The pilgrim eventually returns home—and it's not always an easy transition, especially after the pilgrim has received the Anointing.

Are there any gifts I took home with me after such an experience?

There are—and they've come as a surprise.

I feel a loss of fear.

I feel a loss of anxiety.

I feel an eternal connection to Israel, as though it will be a source of everlasting energy for me.

I feel Jerusalem is a new home I can take with me, wherever I am.

I feel an expanded sense of joy. I experience it as a form of a prayer but one of continuous rejoicing.

I feel that I experienced the Kingdom of God; that I was infused with it; that I really felt it, tasted it, heard it, breathed it, and saw it.

All these gifts have become, for me, the Jerusalem dream.

The Ethiopian Secret

It was at a lecture series on Ethiopia at the Addis Ababa Hilton Hotel that a Catholic priest suggested to his audience of foreign aid workers—secular and nonsecular, consultants, missionaries, teachers, aid workers, etc.— to do themselves a big favor while they were living in Ethiopia.

"While you are here," he said, "be *converted* by the Ethiopian people. We Westerners think we know God. We Westerners think we have God in our pockets. Since I have been here, I have learned otherwise. I have learned who God really is—yes, in this land, in Ethiopia, from Ethiopians.

"It is not a mistake that you are here. I believe people called into this country are also called to go out and share what they've learned with the world."

A chill ran down my spine when I heard his words. He was saying what I had secretly suspected, and quietly observed, during my time there.

"Those of us in the West—in the USA, for sure— think Jesus has brought us prosperity, a nation that cannot fail, a golden path to heaven," the priest continued. "The Ethiopians understand that Jesus brought one thing to the world, and that is God.

"We have missed this simple point. Instead, we have made a big business out of studying Jesus. We debate his historical biography. We have parsed his teachings and in the process have caused so many splits within the church, all claiming they know the true way.

"Meanwhile, the Ethiopians have kept quiet. They have not changed anything. All along, the Ethiopians have known that the key is just to *pray* one's life into heaven.

"I would suggest to you that they have received the Anointing. And so it is said that 'Ethiopia will raise its arm to God.' They have always known that spiritual creation lies in understanding the Tabernacle and that the Old Testament helps us see the full revelation of the New.

"Do not go home without bringing this gift with you."

Questions to Take Home

Having received the Anointing, having received more than I ever expected from my pilgrimage, I left Jerusalem with yet more questions:

How would this experience change my life?

Was there more to receiving the peak experience in the Ethiopian monastery—that is, would it bring further changes to my life?

Would the pilgrimage change my vocation or life focus in a major way?

The fact is, a pilgrimage does not end when you return home. The return home is just the beginning of the next phase of the pilgrimage.

PART FIVE

Epilogue

A DNA Test

After only a few days at home back on Florida's Treasure Coast, I realized that I felt a deep sense of connection to Jerusalem, that the city held an extra-special attraction for me.

I had never felt that sensation before. I had traveled throughout a good portion of the world, and I'd certainly enjoyed many of the places I'd visited, but I'd never before felt that my whole being was tied to any one place.

I felt that there had to be a larger explanation for this feeling—something more than the fact that I'd just been on a pilgrimage there, that I'd visited Jerusalem.

It was a step I had to take: I ordered a DNA fingerprint test from DNA Consultants, Phoenix, AZ. A few weeks later, Dr. Donald Yates called to announce that my report was on its way—and that yes, the Star of David was imprinted on my head, and there are markers for ancestral Jewish DNA in my bloodstream.

When he pronounced his findings, when he said those words, my life changed. It was as if my awareness of this new identity had helped me make sense of my entire life. It certainly explained my extreme attraction to Jerusalem.

A Life Explained

Now the pilgrimage to Israel escalated into a major life event.

It gave me a new identity.

It suggested a new vocation.

It explained all my past intensity: my sense of passion when I was in Ethiopia, my zeal for learning about the Ark of the Covenant and seeing the Tabernacle.

It explained my love for the Ethiopian church, which understands that Christianity is the means by which Judaism's covenant with God attains its intended telos.

It explained why, when I returned home from Ethiopia, I found myself lecturing about the Ethiopian Christian experience, about the meaning of the Ark of the Covenant for Christians, about the meaning of the Tabernacle. Often I would speak on these topics in the presence of Catholic bishops, wondering if they would be open to such discussions.

It also explained my continual feeling that something was missing in Western Christianity.

A Life Changed

The results of the DNA test offered an explanation for my life's passions. It was also responsible for my emerging new vocation.

I began to realize that, unknowingly, I had been teaching and lecturing more and more about the importance of not losing contact with the Old Testament, not erasing the Jewish roots in our Christian experience.

Now not only were my experiences with the pilgrimage and my previous interests and activities pointing to an emerging vocation in this area, but a DNA test was pointing that way as well.

I took these developments very seriously. I prayed for guidance.

What's next? I wondered.

What's Next?

The recent events in my life gave me a renewed sense of purpose. I began to study Biblical Judaism. I researched trends in Christian thought regarding the Old Testament and its role in our Christian heritage.

From that research, a new world emerged: that of Messianic Judaism.

The basic premise of Messianic Judaism is that we Westerners have divorced ourselves so much from the basic roots of Christianity that what is left is a "rupture in need of healing."

The more I read, the more I learned. Could it be true, I wondered, that the term *ecclesia* in the Bible refers to Messianic Judaism and Christian Church, that the full realization of the Christian experience has not yet been fully attained because we have deleted the roots of Christianity?

As I was immersed in reading and research, I was watching ISIS grow. The media were buzzing about what to do and whether we have a strategy.

Meanwhile, I could see the entire global situation arise out of scripture. If we exclude Judaism from our Christian experience, we fail to recognize the *truth* about our current world politics. If we separate the two, we fail to see a world at war, the struggle between the Light and the Dark. If we fail to understand Biblical Judaism, we fail to recognize the pivotal role of Israel in this crisis.

My continued readings suggested that Jews do not believe in Christ but do believe in obedience to the Torah and that Christians do not believe in the Torah but do believe in Christ. We must realize that the present doctrine of the church is inadequate.

It was as if everything I had experienced in Ethiopia, with the amazing fullness of Christianity there, and then everything I'd experienced in Jerusalem, was urging me to take my studies more seriously.

Most amazing has been my encounter with the Queen of Sheba; the fact that she, a woman, stands with Christ at the peak time of biblical history, the Judgment, points to the fact that we must capture the great importance of women throughout biblical history. The Bible in its fullness cannot stand without understanding the theology of woman. After all, the New Testament begins with a woman.

To understand the times we live in, it is necessary to comprehend what we could call the Daughter of Zion. Without her we are unprepared, we cannot grasp the immensity of the biblical accounts.

Lastly, when we understand that ultimately the experience of the Tabernacle is to experience the Mother of God giving birth to her son, the ultimate peak experience, the Anointing, we know that we have encountered a deeper mystery than many would have dreamed possible while here on this earth: we have encountered heaven on earth.

And so my life had changed.

I find myself called to continue to explore the indispensable theology of woman and its essential importance to our full grasp of the Christian experience.

The Jerusalem Dream

My new life had emerged, with a more focused purpose. My life was now the Jerusalem Dream. My purpose was to share this story, to tell my life experience.

We reach this fullness—this Kingdom of God—when we realize that Christianity is the means by which the Judaic covenant with God attains its fulfillment. And when we teach this message unceasingly, the Gospel takes on a resonance so magnificent that it literally gives us the feeling of being born again.

Reaching this fullness means truly understanding Yeshua when he said he did not come to abolish the law but to fulfill it. Continuing the current Christian notion of replacement theology—the notion that we do not need Judaism or to deny the immense role of women in biblical history—will impede our coming to a full joy in Christ.

And so, once upon a time, a pilgrim started out on a journey with the Tabernacle as a guide to the Holy

Land. She did not just arrive home with souvenirs. She returned home to learn of her true identity; she returned home with a new awakening that needs to be shared; she returned home as the Jerusalem Dream.

For more information about

The Jerusalem Dream

Living the Jerusalem Dream

or

Club Jerusalem

visit

_____